Let's Find Ads on Food Packages

by Mari Schuh

first step nonfiction

Lerner Publications ◆ Minneapolis

LERNER

SOURCE

Expand learning beyond the printed book. Download free, complementary educational resources for this book from our website, www.lerneresource.com.

The images in this book are used with the permission of: © Sara Stathas/Alamy, p. 4; © Geri Lavrov/Moment Mobile/Getty Images, p. 5; © Glow Images/Getty Images, p. 6; © Dorann Weber/ Getty Image, pp. 7, 11; © Kristoffer Tripplaar/Alamy, p. 8; © Zero Creatives/Getty Images, p. 9; © iStockphoto.com/Christopher Futcher, p. 10; © Michael Neelon/Alamy, p. 12; James F. Quinn/ Chicago Tribune/Newscom, p. 13; AP Photo/Paul Sakuma, p. 14; © Tim Boyle/Bloomberg/Getty Images, p. 15; Richard B. Levine/Newscom, p. 16; © Todd Strand/Independent Picture Service, p. 17; © Karen Bleier/AFP/Getty Images, p. 18; © iStockphoto.com/Danilin, p. 19; © Michael Neelon/ Alamy, p. 20; © Todd Strand/Independent Picture Service, p. 21; © Brad Wilson/Getty Images, p. 22. Front cover: © XinXinXing/Getty Images.

Main body text set in ITC Avant Garde Gothic Std Medium 21/25.
Typeface provided by International Typeface Corp.

Lerner Publications Company
A division of Lerner Publishing Group, Inc.
241 First Avenue North
Minneapolis, MN 55401 USA

For reading levels and more information, look up this title at www.lernerbooks.com.

Library of Congress Cataloging-in-Publication Data

The Cataloging-in-Publication Data for *Let's Find Ads on Food Packages* is on file at the Library of Congress.
ISBN 978-1-4677-9468-8 (lib. bdg.)
ISBN 978-1-4677-9657-6 (pbk.)
ISBN 978-1-4677-9658-3 (EB pdf)

Manufactured in the United States of America
1 – CG – 12/31/15

Table of Contents

Food and Ads

Food often comes in **packages**.

Many packages have **ads**.

An ad tells these shoppers this food is all natural.

Ads tell **shoppers** about the **product**.

Ads can have words and pictures.

Many ads use bright colors.

An ad can make someone want to buy a product.

Companies use ads to sell their products.

Ads can tell about the food in the package.

Some ads say the food is healthy.

Some ads say the food is easy to make.

Some ads tell people how much food is inside.

Ads can also tell people about other products.

This ad tells people about a soccer game.

Ads can tell people about sports games.

Some ads tell people about movies.

The toy in this meal advertises *Star Wars*.

Sometimes packages have free toys. The toy is an ad.

Ads don't always tell the truth.

CLASSIC FAVORITES

Spaghetti with **Meat Sauce**

tender spaghetti in a
zesty meat sauce with
onions, mushrooms &
tomatoes

How does this food look different from the package?

Some ads make food look better than it is.

Made with **Real** Vegetables

Roasted Vegetable Snacker *Crackers*

Ⓤ Pareve

ENLARGED TO SHOW TEXTURE
SERVING SUGGESTION

NET WT 14.6 OZ (414g)

How much salt is in these vegetable crackers?

Many ads don't tell everything about a product.

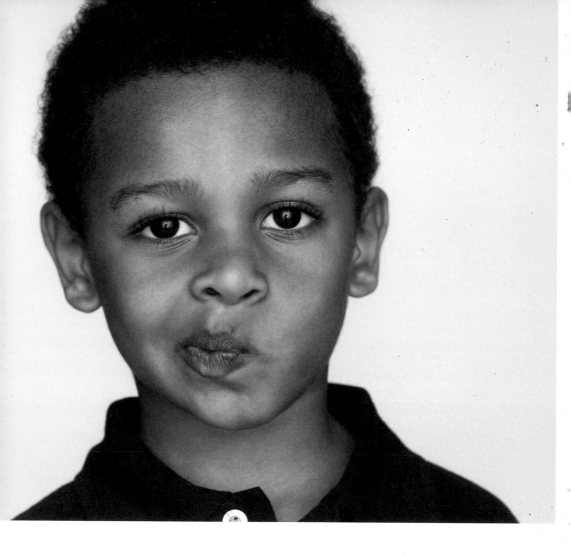

It's smart to ask questions about ads.